The boy Who bit Picasso

The boy Who bit Picasso

Antony PenRose

Abrams Books for Young Readers
New York

My name is **Tony**.

When I was a little boy, living on a farm in East Sussex, England, I had the most extraordinary friend. He had deep black eyes, a big wide smile, and absolutely amazing hands. His hands were absolutely amazing because he could make **paintings** and drawings and **sculptures** and collAgEs and pots and PLATES and much, much more.

Black Face, ceramic, 1948

My friend's name was

Pablo Picasso

and he was one of the

greatest

artists

who ever lived.

Portrait of Lee Miller à l'Arlésienne, 1937

Detail of portrait

My mom, Lee Miller

When Picasso first met my mother, he thought she was so *beautiful* he painted her picture. My friends were very rude about the painting. They thought she looked so ugly she was scary! But actually it was a very good painting.

I discovered that if I took a PHOTOGRAPH of my mother and drew around her face, my drawing fit Picasso's painting exactly—except for her chin. That's because in Picasso's picture she has a huge toothy grin.

Picasso near our home

I lived with Mom and Dad at Farley Farm in Chiddingly.

Picasso was from Spain, but he lived in France.
One day he came all the way from France to visit
my family and me in England.

Drawings by my friend Luke Veevers

England
(Where I live)

France
(Where Picasso lived when he was older)

Spain
(Where Picasso was born and grew up)

Here is me (right), a friend, and my dog, along with Picasso and my mom.

Mom was a PHOTOGRAPHER.

She took most of the photos in this book.

My dad, Roland Penrose, and Picasso

Dad was an **ARTIST**. When Picasso arrived at our farm, the first thing he wanted to see was Dad's studio. The studio was in an old building. It had a big wooden easel to rest **paintings** on.

Picasso liked my dad's studio, but he *really* loved animals. Right away he said he wanted to see the cows and meet our Ayrshire bull . . .

Two Young Bulls, 1945

Our bull's name was **William**.

He was very big but friendly, and he got along really well with Picasso. He liked it when Picasso scratched his ears and talked to him in French.

That evening Picasso sat by the fire and drew William and two of his friends dressed up as flying grasshoppers!

Grasshopper Bulls, 1950

1.11.62.
IV

A drawing by Picasso of a horse that looks a lot like my horse, Gypsy, 1962

Me and Picasso

My teddy bear also liked Picasso.

I couldn't speak French or Spanish, but it didn't matter at all because we didn't need a language for our games. Picasso was great fun to play with. He liked to romp around on the floor and have pretend bullfights. His tweed jacket was nice and scratchy. He smelled good, too. He smelled of cologne and French tobacco.

I don't remember this, but Mom told everyone that one day, when we were playing, I got overexcited and I naughtily bit Picasso.

Me biting Picasso, drawn by Saskia Praill; animals drawn by Luke Veevers

Picasso turned around and
bit me right back—hard!

Just before I started to yell,
Mom heard Picasso say, in
French, "Gosh! That's the first
Englishman I've ever bitten!"

We had a lot of fun with Picasso on our farm,
but eventually it was time for him to go home to
France, where he had four children of his own.

The oldest was a boy named Paulo.

The next oldest was a girl named Maya.

The next next oldest was a boy named Claude
(he was the same age as me).

The youngest was a little girl named Paloma.

Claude (hiding behind one of his father's ceramics) and Paloma

Françoise Gilot with Paloma and Claude, 1951

Picasso loved to draw and **paint** his children as they played while their mother watched.

Claude and Paloma's mother was named Françoise Gilot. She was very kind and gave us *delicious* chocolate treats to eat when we went to visit.

Claude and his mom, Françoise Gilot

Maya with a Doll, 1938

Picasso painted this **picture** of Maya and her doll.

Some of his **Sculptures** look as if he made them as toys.

Man, Woman and Two Children, c.1954, by Françoise Gilot

Françoise was also a good **ARTIST**
and liked to draw her family.

Woman Carrying a Child, 1953

Not long after Picasso had been to our farm,
I heard that my dad was going to visit him in
France, so I gave Dad my little toy London bus
as a present for Claude.

When my dad came back, he brought me a
present from Claude. It was a LITTLE WOMAN
that Picasso had made out of a TINY piece of
wood. I loved her and I put her in charge of
my Noah's Ark to take care of all the animals.

My Noah's Ark set

Claude's gift to me:
Mrs. Noah, c. 1952

Me (I'm six years old now) and Picasso

One day we all went to Vallauris, in the south of France, to visit Picasso. His house wasn't very big, so he used an old perfume factory nearby as a *studio*. I wish I could remember if it still smelled of perfume. Picasso made lots of things in his studio, including a life-size metal lady, which he showed me. He gave her a pretty hat and stuck on a pair of funny eyes.

The sculpture is called *Woman with a Key (The Madame)*, 1954.

An old friend of Picasso's also came to visit. His name was Georges Braque, and he was a famous artist, too. Picasso gave Braque some doves he had made out of **pottery**.

Dove, 1953

Picasso at work in his studio

Picasso did not often use precious materials like gold
or silver. Instead he used the things he found around
him—things you might see in your garden or kitchen
at home. He made this baby out of bits of broken pots.

He liked the pottery baby so much he made her
a **mother** and a carriage as well.

Woman with Baby Carriage, 1950

Picasso in his studio

Picasso also made this **sculpture** of a little girl skipping.
Look at her feet. Doesn't she look as if she's wearing
her mother's shoes?

Picasso and his pet monkey

At one time Picasso had a pet monkey. I never met the monkey … but I did see the sculpture Picasso made of a monkey mother with her baby.

Take a look at the mother's face. Can you see what Picasso used to make it? He used Claude's toy car.

Baboon and Young, 1951

Eventually Picasso's house became too small, so he moved to a bigger one in a nearby town called Cannes. He filled his new house with strange musical instruments, African masks, birds in cages, magazines and maps, bits of junk, and of course lots of things he had made.

"Has Picasso just moved in?" I asked my mother when we went to visit.

"No," she replied. "He's been here quite a long time. Why do you ask?"

"Well, he hasn't put his things away," I said.

"That's how he likes it," she said with a laugh.

Me and Picasso's parrot

Picasso loved having fun and he let us children play with things, but he got very upset with adults if they touched anything.

However, as much as Picasso loved having fun, he also worked and worked and worked.

He was always *experimenting,*

always inventing,

always making things.

Picasso kept lots of his sculptures in his house and garden. He made them from *junk*, which he transformed into **ART**. Can you see the nanny goat in the photo below? Picasso used an old basket to make her tummy, and a palm-tree branch to make her backbone. The nanny goat looked so alive I thought she was Esmeralda's mother . . .

Picasso's garden

Esmeralda the goat and Patsy, my nanny

Goat's Head in Profile, ceramic, 1952

Esmeralda was Picasso's pet goat. Here she is, talking to my nanny, Patsy.

Esmeralda slept in a crate outside Picasso's bedroom door. I thought this was great. At home I was never allowed to bring the farm animals inside the house.

Dove, date unknown

Picasso also kept doves. He built nesting boxes for them around his bedroom windows. He used to leave the windows open so they could fly into the room and peck at seed he left on the floor. They pooped all over the floor and sometimes on the bed, but he didn't mind at all!

Here is a **picture** Picasso painted of the sunny bay of Cannes, seen from his bedroom window. Can you see some doves sitting quietly in their nesting boxes?

The Pigeons, Cannes, 1957

It wasn't always quiet in Picasso's house, though.
In fact it was often like a carnival. Picasso loved
disguises. Can you see which bits of his face are
false?

He kept a side table piled high with masks and funny hats. We all had to choose a disguise and wear it for most of the day. Can you see me here?

I'm now nine years old (that's me with Picasso, in case my disguise fooled you).

Even Mom used to dress up. She must have liked her new nose because she took this PHOTO of herself in the mirror . . .

Young Wood Owl, 1952

Meanwhile, Picasso became more and more famous, like a rock star or a baseball player today. But people began to bother him too much, so he moved to another house, in a town called Vauvenargues, that was more private.

Picasso and my dad

One time my dad visited Picasso by himself, and that's when something special happened. Picasso asked about me, and my dad explained that I was unhappy because I had been sent to a very strict school to make sure I passed my exams. Picasso thought this was a terrible idea!

To cheer me up he sent me a little drawing. It showed a bull watching a dancer playing a flute, with a centaur listening. The drawing has cheered me up ever since.

Bull, Centaur and Dancing Figure Playing Pipes, 1960

Picasso carried on creating art for many, many years. When he eventually died, at the ripe old age of 91, he left behind him nearly **2,000** paintings, more than **7,000** drawings, well over **1,000** sculptures, and much, much more. Today he is one of the most famous artists in the world . . . but to me he will always be my most extraordinary friend, and I hope he is now yours, too.

Illustration Credits

All the artwork is by Pablo Picasso unless otherwise noted in the captions. Photographs are by Lee Miller unless otherwise noted.

Corgi® **p. 24 above** Picture provided by Corgi® registered trademark of Hornby Hobbies Ltd.

Françoise Gilot **p. 23 right** *Man, Woman and Two Children*, c. 1954. © Françoise Gilot, 2010. All rights reserved.

Lee Miller **p. 2** Antony Penrose and Odette Himmuel, Farley Farm House, East Sussex, England, 1949 (original untinted); **p. 4** Antony Penrose gardening, Farley Farm House, East Sussex, England, c. 1952; **p. 7** Picasso, Villa La Californie, Cannes, France, 1957; **p. 9 right** Self-portrait, New York Studio, New York, USA, 1932 (with outline added); **p. 10** Picasso by signpost, Chiddingly, East Sussex, England, 1950; **p. 13 above** Roland Penrose and Picasso, Farley Farm House, East Sussex, England, 1950; **p. 14** Picasso, Antony Penrose and William the bull, Farley Farm House, East Sussex, England, 1950; **p. 17** Picasso and Antony Penrose, Farley Farm House, East Sussex, England, 1950; **p. 20** Claude and Paloma Picasso with Picasso ceramic, Vallauris, France, 1953; **p. 21 below** Claude Picasso and Françoise Gilot, Vallauris, France, 1949; **p. 26** Picasso and Antony Penrose beside *Woman with a Key (The Madame)*, Vallauris, France, 1954; **p. 27** Antony Penrose and Picasso, Vallauris, France, 1954; **pp. 28–29** Picasso and Georges Braque, Vallauris, France, 1954; **p. 30** Picasso making sculpture, Vallauris, France, 1954; **p. 32** Picasso and sculpture, Vallauris, France, 1954; **p. 34** Antony Penrose with Picasso's parrot, Notre Dame de Vie, France, 1962; **p. 35** Picasso's studio, Villa La Californie, Cannes, France, 1957; **pp. 36–37** Picasso playing his African xylophone, Villa La Californie, Cannes, France, 1957; **p. 38** Château de Vauvenargues, France, c. 1960; **p. 39 above** Patsy Murray and Esmeralda, Villa La Californie, Cannes, France, 1956; **p. 42** Picasso in mask, Villa La Californie, Cannes, France, 1957; **p. 43** Antony Penrose in mask with Picasso, Villa La Californie, Cannes, France, 1956; **p. 44** Self-portrait with mask, Villa La Californie, Cannes, France, 1956; **p. 46** Picasso and Roland Penrose, Villa La Californie, Cannes, France, 1956. © Lee Miller Archives, England 2010. All rights reserved.

Antony Penrose **p. 24 below, pp. 24–25** Photographs © Antony Penrose, England 2010. All rights reserved.

Roland Penrose **p. 12** Picasso, Lee Miller and Antony Penrose with friend, Farley Farm House, East Sussex, England, 1950 (original untinted); **p. 33 above** Picasso with a monkey, Antibes, France, 1939. © Roland Penrose Archives, England 2010. All rights reserved.

Pablo Picasso **p. 1** *Head of a Faun*, 1948; **p. 5** *Black Face*, 1948; **p. 8, p. 9 left** *Portrait of Lee Miller à l'Arlesienne*, 1937 (and detail, with outline added); **p. 13 below** *Two Young Bulls*, 1945; **p. 15** *Grasshopper Bulls*, design from the visitors' book of the Institute of Contemporary Arts, London, 1950; **p. 16** *Horse*, 1962; **p. 21 above** *Françoise Gilot with Paloma and Claude*, 1951; **p. 22** *Maya with a Doll*, 1938; **p. 23 left** *Woman Carrying a Child*, 1953; **p. 24 below** *'Mrs Noah'*, c. 1952; **p. 29** *Dove*, 1953; **p. 31** *Woman with Baby Carriage*, 1950; **p. 33 below** *Baboon and Young*, 1951; **p. 39 below** *Goat's Head in Profile*, 1952; **p. 40** *Dove*, date unknown; **p. 41** *The Pigeons*, Cannes, 1957; **p. 45** *Young Wood Owl*, 1952; **p. 47** *Bull, Centaur and Dancing Figure Playing Pipes*, 1960 © Succession Picasso/DACS 2010

Saskia Praill (aged 11) **p. 18 and cover**

Katya Sanigar (aged 6½) **p. 1, p. 3** hand-lettering

Luke Veevers (aged 11) **p. 6, p. 11, p. 19, p. 48**

For Kahina and Tarik, with my love —A. P.

My beloved horse, Gypsy, by Luke Veevers

The author would like to thank Ami Bouhassane, Carole Callow, Paul Davis, Lance Downie, Victoria Fenton, Laura Green, Kate Henderson, Gabi Hergert, Tracy Leeming, Brenda Longley, Kerry Negahban, and Stephanie Wooller, all at Farley Farm House (www.farleyfarmhouse.co.uk).

Cataloging-in-Publication Data has been applied for and may be obtained from the Library of Congress.
ISBN 978-0-8109-9728-8

First published in the United Kingdom in 2010 by
Thames & Hudson Ltd,
181A High Holborn,
London WC1V 7QX

www.thamesandhudson.com

The Boy Who Bit Picasso © 2010 Antony Penrose

Printed and bound in China
10 9 8 7 6 5 4 3 2 1

Abrams Books for Young Readers are available at special discounts when purchased in quantity for premiums and promotions as well as fundraising or educational use. Special editions can also be created to specification. For details, contact specialmarkets@abramsbooks.com or the address below.

ABRAMS
THE ART OF BOOKS SINCE 1949

115 West 18th Street
New York, NY 10011
www.abramsbooks.com

Glossary

Art: objects, environments, or experiences created through the use of skill and imagination that can be shared with others and that appeal to the senses or emotions

Artist: a person who creates art

Braque, Georges (1882–1963): a major twentieth-century French painter and sculptor who, along with Pablo Picasso, developed the art style known as Cubism

Ceramics: the practice of making objects—such as tiles, bricks, containers, plates, and other tableware—out of clay and similar materials, then heating them to a high temperature to preserve them. See *Pottery*.

Collage: an assemblage of different forms (such as paper, photographs, and found objects) to create a new whole

Disguise: to change one's appearance with a costume or other means of deception so that one's true identity is hidden

Drawing: a representation by lines of an object or idea, made with pen, pencil, etc.

Junk: anything that is regarded as worthless, meaningless, or trash

Mask: an object that, when used, disguises or conceals something meant to be hidden

Painting: a picture or design made by applying pigment, color, or another medium to a surface

Photograph: an image, especially a print, recorded by a camera and reproduced on a photosensitive surface

Photographer: a person who takes photographs using a camera

Picture: a visual representation of a person, object, or scene, such as a painting, drawing, photograph, etc.

Pottery: objects of a certain shape—such as pots and tableware—formed by clay and then heated to a high temperature to preserve them. See *Ceramics*.

Sculpture: a three-dimensional figurative or abstract artwork created by carving, modeling, welding, or other means

Studio: an artist's workroom

Where you can see the work of Pablo Picasso

CANADA
Art Gallery of Ontario
National Gallery of Canada, Ottawa

UNITED STATES

California
Fine Arts Museums of San Francisco,
    California Palace of the Legion of Honor
Los Angeles County Museum of Art
Norton Simon Museum, Pasadena
San Francisco Museum of Modern Art

Connecticut
Yale University Art Gallery, New Haven

Illinois
Art Institute of Chicago

Maryland
Baltimore Museum of Art

Massachusetts
Harvard Art Museum/Fogg Art Museum,
    Cambridge
Museum of Fine Arts, Boston

New York
Guggenheim Museum, New York City
Metropolitan Museum of Art, New York City
Museum of Modern Art, New York City

Ohio
Cleveland Museum of Art
Toledo Museum of Art

Pennsylvania
Barnes Foundation, Philadelphia
Philadelphia Museum of Art

Texas
Kimbell Art Museum, Fort Worth
Modern Art Museum of Fort Worth

Washington, D.C.
Hirshhorn Museum and Sculpture Garden
National Gallery of Art
Phillips Collection

Antony's parents were **Lee Miller** and **Sir Roland Penrose**. Lee Miller (1907–1977) was a celebrated Surrealist photographer and produced some of the most powerful photographs of the twentieth century, from portraits of her friends (including Pablo Picasso), to her work as a correspondent with the United States Army during World War II, to her work with *Vogue* magazine. She is best remembered for her witty Surrealist images. Her photographs are held in a number of permanent collections, including those of the Art Institute of Chicago and the New Orleans Museum of Art.

Sir Roland Penrose (1900–1984) was an English Surrealist painter and poet best known for his exhibitions and books on the work of his friends Pablo Picasso, Max Ernst, Joan Miró, Man Ray, and Antoni Tàpies. He organized the International Surrealist Exhibition of 1936, which led to the establishment of an English Surrealist movement. Sir Roland is best known for his postcard collages, examples of which are found in major national collections worldwide, including those of the Art Institute of Chicago and the New Orleans Museum of Art.

Antony's friend was **Pablo Picasso** (1881–1973), a Spanish painter and sculptor. He is best known for cofounding Cubism and for the stylistic range of his work. His artistic accomplishments made him one of the best-known figures in twentieth-century art.

Cubism is a style of painting, collage, and sculpture initiated in the early twentieth century by Pablo Picasso and Georges Braque. It portrayed objects and natural forms (such as houses, furniture, people, and animals) as multifaceted geometrical shapes.

Surrealism is a twentieth-century literary and artistic movement that attempts to express the workings of the subconscious (sometimes imagined as a dreamlike world or thoughts) and is characterized by fantastic imagery and unexpected or absurd combinations of subject matter.